COLLECTED POEMS

COLLECTED POEMS

Barry Sheinkopf

*with a Foreword by
Dan Balaban*

*Full Court Press
Englewood Cliffs, New Jersey*

First Edition

Copyright © 1973, 1985, 1993, 1998, 1999, 2002, 2009
by Barry Sheinkopf

All rights reserved. No part of this book may be reproduced or transmitted in any form or by any means electronic or mechanical, including by photocopying, by recording, or by any information storage and retrieval system, without the express permission of the author and publisher, except where permitted by law.

Published in the United States of America
by Full Court Press, 601 Palisade Avenue
Englewood Cliffs, NJ 07632

ISBN 978-1-60743-861-8

Library of Congress Control No. 2009902117

Some of these poems have appeared in the Bergen Jewish News, Surface Design, Innesfree, and Saints+Sinners, and are gratefully acknowledged

*Editing and Book Design by Barry Sheinkopf
or www.bookshapers.com*

Author Photograph by Barrow Davis

Cover Photograph, "Bamboo Grove, Stonecrop Gardens, Cold Spring, NY," Copyright © 2008 Barry Sheinkopf

Foreword Copyright © 2009 Dan Balaban

Full Court Press Colophon by Liz Sedlack

For Eugenia,
and for Susan and David
Without whom nothing

*Any brute
can buy a machine in a shop,
but the sacred spells are secret to the kind,
and if power is what we wish
they won't work.*

—W.H. Auden

Foreword

Barry Sheinkopf is a real poet, the genuine article. One realizes it immediately. His mentor, W.H. Auden, can step from his fairly recent tomb, lock right arm through his disciple's left, and wander the poetic landscape in collegial exchange. Sheinkopf's *Collected Poems* is that good.

He ranges like a net, collecting news items, love poems, story poems, stray thoughts, whatever. Often he shifts abruptly to a spectral tone, as at the end of "The Wave":

> I rode
> the rising wind
> and we
>
> were so alone
> together,
> so adrift

He offers astonishing reveries. In "Nones," a painting of a river in Holland is described; Watteau and Breughel comment on an aspect of the sky above it. Sheinkopf disagrees with them, tells why, then encapsulates the episode as "...a painting / next to a painting."

He's a poet who tells stories. There are three here—"After They Shot Poor John Wilkes Booth," "The Counterfeiter's Tale," and "The Pearl"—in which he seems to have acquired the subject matter from others, then researched and produced them. Each is dazzlingly narrated, the poet in full pursuit.

When he turns to nature, Sheinkopf's power and originality are piercing. "Inchoate Sunshine Cannot Tell" is a brief masterpiece reproduced here in full:

Inchoate sunshine cannot tell
you if your heart and mind are well,
compelled instead to merely pour
on bodies from the latest war
and teams on mountain tops alike.
It feels no urge to start a strike
or want to gladden, yet it does—
its only language for what was,
the shale-preserved imprint of rain,
the xylic stamp of every strain
in Joshua trees as old as words,
it opens up the throats of birds.

Also to be singled out is the complex contemplation of 9/11/2001 entitled "Not to Put Too Fine a Point on It."

To interpose a quibble in so fine a collection, the first page of "Man Who Played Piano" sketches the life of the great piano player Bill Evans. The rest of it is an ode to him and, to my mind, should have been presented as a separate poem.

What remains is to hail Barry Sheinkopf as the great poet he is. Along with experiencing a fine talent, one savors appealing garlicky traces of a morose take on the world.

—*Dan Balaban*

Preface

I never imagined, as these poems were being written, that I would ever finish enough of them, or live long enough, to produce a *Collected Poems*. That I have managed to do both is a testament largely to those upon whose love I have depended.

All good poems are exercises in having your cake and eating it—expressing at once, that is, something true and cadenced and heartfelt—*and* designing what W.H. Auden liked to call a "verbal toy." In my own case, since I was trained young in the mechanics of prosody but have spent most of my life in a world in which artifice is almost universally, if naively, looked down upon as a denial of authenticity, this toy has frequently appeared as a sonnet, ballad, or some French or Italianate form that doesn't seem like a *form* when you read it but like free verse. *Not That I Minded,* and a good deal of *Live From The Limelight,* turned on that obsession. In *Email,* I was taken by a similar hunger: to see if it was possible to write clear poems with almost no punctuation (since that does seem to be what writing is going to look like in the future). It is of course nutty to be taken by such formal concerns, but goals in poetry are always nutty; if they weren't, you could make a business out of them.

I've also aimed to write poems that say something intelligible and to tear up those that don't, which is not easy, since so few, all in all, remain. But that is as it should be. I agree with Auden when he says in *About the House,* one of his finest collections,

> *Even a limerick*
> *ought to be something a man of*
> *honor, awaiting death from cancer or a firing squad,*
> *could read without contempt*

Far too many contemporary poems fail that test miserably; whatever their postmodernist justification, they seem to me empty of consequence, shells without fish.

I'd love to write some more poems before, as John Mortimer put it, I fall off the twig (I'd certainly have it written of me on my urn that I was a poet, of which I am prouder than I am of anything else I have ever written), but who knows? I'm hedging my bets here, gathering all the poems I wish to preserve in one place so none will be thrown out with old copies of the *New Yorker*. Some of these efforts have achieved a little notoriety; I have read most of them in scores of public appearances over the years and often found they pleased.

They're as short as I could make them. There would be more of them if I hadn't got it into my head at one point to write poems that were so short they contained no words at all, and been thus drawn to the still camera—I invariably see certain lights and shadows, certain breath-stopping shapes, that make it hard to choose. But as the young now say, whatever; I hope you like what there is.

—B.S.,
West New York, 2009

Table of Contents

Not That I Minded

A Roof of Birds, *1*

Arousal, *2*

Dyad, *5*

Elegy for Patrick, *7*

Friend of Mine, *11*

Harbingers of the New Life, *13*

Inchoate Sunshine Cannot Tell, *14*

Le Livre de M'Amie, *15*

Limericks, *16*

Lovesong, *17*

Man Who Played Piano, *19*

March Morning, *23*

Morton Street Pier, *24*

Nones, *26*

Not to Have Failed, *29*

November, *30*

O Thank You, Lord, *32*

Others, *34*

Precis, *35*

Prose and the Passion, *36*

Ready or Not, *48*

Sacre du Printemps, *51*

Sext, 52

Tambourine, 54

The Approach, 56

The Wave, 58

This Poem Noise, 60

Vespers, 61

We Knew Each Other, 62

West River Sundown, 63

Live From The Limelight

Sex May Be Easy, But Passion Takes Class, 67

After They Shot Poor John Wilkes Booth, 69

The Stars These Days, 77

These College Girls, 79

The Counterfeiter's Tale, 81

Tisha B'av Follies, 91

Thin Air, 95

The Pearl, 96

Kid on a Bike, 101

Christ Church Cemetery, Philadelphia, 102

Raining, 103

No Luck at All, 105

Spring Cleaning, 110

Come Again?, 111

Confession, 116

Email: Poems in Real Time

Brighter Now, *119*

Hot to Trot, *121*

A Pal, *122*

Passing in the Hall, *123*

Pedal to the Metal, *125*

From the Poetry License Bureau, *126*

Plat du Jour, *127*

Soon You Will Forget Your Own Name, *129*

Lately the Sunlight on Your Face, *131*

You Get My Business Card, *132*

So Here's What I Tell Her, *134*

Over and Over and Over, *137*

Fat Kid, *138*

Dress Boy, *141*

Not to Put Too Fine a Point on It, *146*

Pasadena Blonde, *153*

What He Never Told Me, *158*

Hot Shiskebab, *163*

What We Were Talking About, *167*

The Girl in the Low-Cut Jeans, *169*

Sometime or Other, *171*

When I Miss You, *173*

Walking Man, *175*

Let Me Suggest the Following, *178*

Tanka, *180*

Two Haiku, *181*

I Want to Thank, *182*

I Keep on Writing Poems, *184*

How Many Times, *185*

*Not That
I Minded*

A Roof of Birds

Daybreak the starlings gather black,
black fists against black branches,
sky as clear as ice.

Strange company to keep.
I pause to find a metaphor;
they clamor to be gone

with all the migrant wishes
stapled to their spars.
The earth is wound

from black silk strands,
from shadowed terrors
waiting to explode—

and then they do, the birds,
as one, driving the heart out,
turning the air to cloth.

AROUSAL

I found you
as one finds
a morning sun

force life
through
frozen grass.

The end
of night's
an ordinary thing,

I know,
though
only those

who have not
torn a fury
through their years

could fail
to be amazed
by such a light

shimmering
through
my tears—

for in the dark
where all my passion,
all the pulse

of what I meant to be
lay whimpering,
content, or worn,

the sun was only
metaphor.
I found you so,

my memory of love
a tranquil thing,
at times

a bitter weed,
but not as if
the morning light

had just begun

to warm the air
along my side.

Last time I left you
feeling
that I knew so much.

Dyad

Entranced,
he waits to see
the spirit move

and feels
her nervous eyes
reprove

his twitching lips,
his worried look.
She knows

about his terror,
how
it shows

each time
he breathes:
her heart

so full—
if only he
would play his part—

of everything
he
used to need;

her arms
a twining tale
that he can't read;

her eyes
like signal fires
in smoky air

he didn't trust
to tell him
she was there.

Elegy for Patrick
(Patrick Kelly Ob. February 22, 1984)

It was dead still the night
that I left you to die,
and the moon seemed to hang
between flights in the sky,

not quite certain it knew
when you wanted to leave.
It was crisp as the stars
when I started to grieve.

The temple I kissed
for the last time (as warm
with the beat of your blood
as the liquidest form

you could cut when you danced
in a white-trousered blur
and the crowd stopped to stare
at the beauty you were)

was sweeter than silk
to my lips. Maybe so;

maybe thus, in thus touching,
you happened to go

from the nearly alive
to a glittering sleep
on the flow of the goodness
you gave me to keep,

as you gave of the best
and the finest of you
for so long, to so many.
The waiting was through;

the doctor said you could
feel nothing but pain
any more, teary-eyed
when she tried to explain.

Then she left, and I pressed
all the love in my soul
to your cheek—for the luck
of the wind, for the roll

of the silver-gray clouds
heading north through the wee

morning hours, just the shade
of your hair. *Let it be,*

cried the voice that preserves,
but my heart needed staying
a while, and my hands
weren't set to obeying,

though what I was waiting
for, God only knows—
one more taste of that easy
sweet love, I suppose—

until, suddenly, even
the air seemed to know:
only that may endure
which is given to go.

So I left, and the spot
on my back, just below
the left shoulder blade,
weightlessly lifted. Oh,

Patrick, dear Patrick,
your houses were still.

your loved ones asleep
in the lingering chill

of the last winter night
that you happened to fill
with your breath and your sight
before joining the dawn with a will—

and the silence exploded
in gathering light,
the silence exploded
in gathering light.

Friend of Mine

She was visiting her neighbor down the hall
sweet old crackpot in his eighties
keeping him company on Christmas Eve
when a guy comes over
guy weighs over three hundred,
calls himself a spiritual healer,
and, after they all had a beer
this maniac fat man
started to punch her out.
He hurt her, she tells me
a couple days later
while we're talking on the phone—
hurt her; her arms and her chest
are still black and blue.
"I was—shit, I was scared,"
she says. "And all this time,
he's saying how much he likes me."

She got out of there
as fast as she could, she says,
but she had to go back.
Couldn't tell what he'd do
to the old man, couldn't tell

if the cops would have put the fat pig away
or not, if she'd called.
"So what happened?" I ask.
"That was it. Seemed to be just fine."
I shake my head. "Jesus," I tell her.
"So what else is new?"
She's writing a piece for a graduate course
on Emerson, Melville, and Hawthorne,
she explains, all about evil and pride
and how you have to see reality
before you dream it. "Jesus," I say
again. "Yeah," she replies.
"Ain't it a pisser, though?"

Harbingers of the New Life

A study recently completed
in San Francisco
into the causes
of teenage auto injuries
has revealed that, yes,
some say that alcohol and driving
do not mix, and some blame drugs
and eating poorly or Not Seeing Doctor
When Ill, but think of it:
One out of every three
women surveyed checked off
Sexual Intercourse as well.

Inchoate Sunshine Cannot Tell

Inchoate sunshine cannot tell
you if your heart and mind are well,
compelled instead to merely pour
on bodies from the latest war
and teams on mountain tops alike.
It feels no urge to start a strike
or want to gladden, yet it does—
its only language for what was,
the shale-preserved imprint of rain,
the xylic stamp of every strain
in Joshua trees as old as words,
it opens up the throats of birds.

Le Livre de M'Amie

Grass will teach you manners:
to greenly eye all flowering things
and conquer by surrounding
what towers above you;

or learn to hold a cup of tea
with grace in the palm of your speech—
especially when words are left unsaid
and the face must improvise,

especially when woods are left fallow
of a leaf's treasure, and you fade.
Be then more fragile and alive
than now in your burst of smile,

and may the sway of grass astound you
always, for when we pause, we are old.

Limericks

1

There was a young woman from Nice
whose hair was like gossamer fleece,
but she wasn't Lautrec
when she ate her *bifteck*
and proceeded to lick up the grease.

2

You cannot begin to express
the things that she does for that dress;
like a customs inspector,
you gotta respect her—
what she don't declare, you can guess.

LOVESONG

Pare it *down*,
I have thought
for the many long years
I've been trying
to write—
pare it down;
there is less
you can say
that is true
than there is
that is false.

Now I study
your face
like a man
who has never
seen day,
who has never
touched something
alive.

I explode
on the lemony curl

of your lips

as you ask

do I love you,

and all

of my heart,

all the words

I can say,

all the millions

of words

in my throat

like a meadow

of stars

in the clearest

of skies

on the darkest

of nights,

are as one

burning syllable:

yes.

Man Who Played Piano
(In Memoriam Bill Evans, ob. September 15, 1980)

There was a man who played piano
sweet as sweet can be,
because a terror in his soul
condemned him to be free,

a terror cold and crisp and dry
that longed so hard for death
that every new leaf opening
could make him catch his breath.

And when he played piano, why,
your heart would skip a beat;
a smile would form across your lips,
a memory, a fleet

remembered hawk in sunlit flight
across a blue sky, bluer
at four o'clock than blue itself,
and maybe even truer.

The trouble was, the terror won,
and that—well, that was jazz.

He crafted afternoons of gold
where everybody has

enough to eat, enough to dream,
enough to love a bird
hurtling across a rural sky.
And everybody heard

a song so effortlessly light
the terror never showed;
they listened and they sighed aloud
and never knew he *owed*:

He owed the lazy voice at night.
He owed the drugs, the booze.
But most of all he owed the love
of dying when you choose.

So Death came calling one fine day
and said to him, "Hey, Bro—
you love my lovin' way too much.
I'm goin' take you slow."

The terror then grew daily worse;
the rapture, too, grew sad,

and he found ways to try to die
he never knew he had.

And then, by God, the agony
that lashed across his face,
the biting chest and stomach pain
that couldn't leave a trace:

two hundred bucks a day on coke
and keyboards on a stage
oceans away, and aching chills,
and dying page by page,

measure for measure, the dull sweep
of a truth across the sky
that will not offer answers
when the question starts with *why*.

But in the end, when Death came back
to finish out the set,
unwilling out of sheer respect
to ask about the debt,

and the doctors puzzled, nervously
frowning, and nurses ran

shaking their heads at the slack mouth
and the still hands of the man

who played a sweet piano, sweet
as sweet ccould be, Death said,
"My man, you somethin' else," and closed
his eyes. "You still ain't dead."

March Morning

Ah, wintry
10 a.m.—
the shadow

of a fat
round tire
reclines

against
Ted Nooley's
bleached garage

(the saddest,
oldest
pink),

against
Ted Nooley's
yellow air jacks,

tailpipes,
and his
bright blue truck.

Morton Street Pier

Nothing remains to be said:
having had her in bed,
having taken his fill
of her heart's sweet will,
he already imagines them wed,

paints pictures in which
nooks are sunny—a switch
from a lonelier plight,
as the candles at night
that hallow the darkly-rich

splendor of her hair.
He's heard of a commonwealth where
such women as she
can actually be
entirely true and fair,

where a life may be lived in peace
(though all worlds someday cease)
and the silentest vow
 right here and now
may endlessly release.

He's heard, but has never known,
life needn't be lived on loan
but pay as you go.
Still, he's happy to know
at last that he's not on his own,

and trying for once to see
if even a sort such as he
can stand by the mast,
daring the vast
kept secrets of the sea,

and manage to somehow find
his port, though the wake behind
churn frantically white
in the dangerous night,
and the reckoning's nearly blind.

Nones

I

The river
is a painting of a river,
greenish gray, dimensionless
as time can be,

done by a painter
off on the last leg
of a rose phase
the major quest of which was Dawn.

Curious how the eye grew fixed,
as if resting in shock
at the merest hint
of a sharp edge in the water—

the way a hull heaved,
pressing sunlight back
against the air. And curious
how the choice resolved itself,

the hand in penitence reclaimed

a beach head wholly built on thought,
the palette drained of whatsoever lies
it formerly had told.

2

Angular, decisive,
two hang-gliders
linger
above the river

as if held up against the sky
by a god
with an easy life:
so high

bystanders
can't make out the feet.
Hang-gliders' feet that are standing
on nothing.

Watteau
could have read that sky
with the clouds marshaled across it
like rosy goldfish scales

that rest along each other or against.
Breughel, too—but the fading pinks
the gliders sail beneath
like lazy hawks

are far too gray for Breughel,
and the windless river
far too kind. They sail
as if come

crash-helmeted
to worlds of fern and fog:
they are a painting
next to a painting.

Not to Have Failed
(for my mother)

You're enraged; I'll also be,
and I pray that my rage
isn't over the things
only I could have managed to miss,

though I naturally know
it won't happen like that.
I'd like my lips, at least, to feel
the way my father's kiss

felt—not to have failed
by stealth or pride
to freely render love,
not to be strangled like this.

November
(for my father)

Any month the trees
Begin to look like praying
Sets of hands, and color
    Bleaches from my eye,
Suddenly I listen
To my father's footsteps
Eerily above me,
    Scraping on the sky.

Forty years have happened
Since the day I left him
Standing at a counter
    In his hat and tie,
Took a plane for somewhere,
Working out my future,
Certain he was only
    Playing he would die.

Any month the awful
Wind comes tearing through me,
Money is a problem,
    Friends have gone and lied,

Quietly I listen
To the creaking branches,
Just as I have listened
    Ever since he died.

O Thank You, Lord

O thank you, Lord,
for pretty things—
the undersides
of robins' wings,

the bark of crisp
December pine,
the heart of flame,
the splendid lines

in a fine old
chest of drawers.
It's good to see
a squirrel yawn.

There's so much
strangled pain
around me, bleeding
into the ground like rain,

like shopworn sleet.
Nothing I sing
will save the starving babies.

I but bring

quite stunned
to your attention
in my cradling hands
what I can hardly mention,

only try to show:
that innocence, though often sad,
endures; that sanity exists
even among the mad.

Others

You'll never know them: Daily they appear,
conduct their daily business, and are gone,
leaving a scent as human and as near
as closer friends do. Time slides on;

you grow accustomed to the clothes they wear,
the kinds of spices that they add to stews,
occasionally learn the things they care
about, the cheap tricks that their children use.

It seems as if you often understand
exactly what they mean to say but don't,
particularly when they need a hand
with something they could ask you for but won't.

They get about as close as TV news
or gifts that you would never think to choose.

Precis

I only try to combine
the passion of summer shade
and of being afraid in bed
at a quarter to nine.

I have no other goals,
no other special plan.
All of my daily needs
must first be met

before a structure reaches
to grapple wintry peaks,
before the eagle seeks
what only the mountain teaches.

Prose and the Passion

Air and moon are still,
especially the moon:
the witching hour
is here again
to stay. Ears soon
adjust to the shrill
ache of the sour
shadows of Then

when some of life
was nearly understood,
mouths dry
in telling tales,
the bird of the night wood
plunges like a knife
through charcoal sky,
and the heart fails.

See that man
with cold light falling on his coat?
His name is Axel, and he's paused
to check his watch. It's later
than he thought; a note
of hesitation thicker than

he'd like—a tremor caused
by Sweet Marie far greater

than his brain can still—
shakes in his wrist
and twitches at his chin.
She's said she'll meet
him, once, that anyone she's kissed,
she says (at least until
the memory of kissing grows too thin),
deserves as much. His feet

have turned to ice, although
it's still as warm as late Septembers
get—and, since he knows what *that*
means, Axel takes a breath,
recalls her liquid form, remembers
how she smelled and felt, and so
much more, trembling at
the edge of life and death

before he moves. She hit him like a brick:
the perfect teeth, the full lips
reaching like a bud for light,
and eyes so hungry after

clues to life, insiders' tips;
she even said, "I want to learn your trick
for staying free when the sight
of your face disgusts you, and the laughter

stops." He tried, knees giving way,
his mug of coffee warm
against his tired skin,
wanting her before
he even knew. He asked, "You want the form?"
and laughed. "Don't have no rules today—
though, anyhow, the shape I'm in
right now, I wouldn't want to bore

you. . . . Passion," he said,
"is haunting. Like another beer?"
"Why not?" She spread her fingers like a fan
and asked him, "Haunting how?"
"Like—oh, like fire," he said. "Like fear.
Like heavy rain on windows in the dead
of March." She slowly ran
a fingernail across her teeth. "Like now?"

He blushed; she laughed; they left
the place together after two more rounds,

and Sweet Marie was sweeter than the sun,
and Axel was as loving as the rain,
and sounds were summer sounds—
abandoned cotton clothing, silk in the cleft
of thigh on glistening thigh, and squeals of fun,
and sighs that neither needed to explain. . . .

Feeling better, Axel hurries
down Thirteenth. Across the street,
a woman snoozes, right
on the heated subway grate
in front of the bank, her broad feet
swollen in rubber shoes. He worries
what he'll tell Marie tonight.
It's nearly five to eight.

Marie, meanwhile, has been applying
a touch of rouge, eye-liner,
color to her mouth. A rising
pressure in her chest
suggests to her she may look finer
than she'd like. Eyeing
her face as he would—sizing
up the lips, the hair, she sees the rest

fall into place like a leaf
on a darkened path, and throws
a sweater on, knowing she's late
but suddenly immersed in heavy thought.
She really doesn't think she owes
him anything. They had, she thinks, a brief
enlightening fling. Then why *await*
him so, and why are the tears caught

in her throat? She shakes
her head, checks keys cash lipstick,
locks the door, and marches out
to meet him. Pumpkins flicker
in windows. God, the guy's so thick,
she nearly says aloud; it takes
her just a second more to shout,
"You see? I'm even *walking* quicker!"

Charley Morton stops to stare,
and his fourteen-year-old terrier Mike stops, too.
She murmurs, "Sorry," quickly smiles; he tips
his cap, and he and Mike
return their fellow-minded gaze to true
gray stone, the street lamp, and the fair
moon shining as it slips

between the clouds like

some remembered face.
"You shouldn't stay out late
tonight!" she hears him calling.
"Yes, I know," she turns to say.
"Oh, Charley, I'm in such a state—
I have to learn to pace
myself a little better. I am falling
on my face too much this way,"

she adds, and shrugs. "My dear, my sweet Marie,"
he says— "only the heart
can slow you down enough
to hear your footsteps," as he shakes
his head. "The only part
of life that counts, the only easy
place where all that bitter stuff
your time is cut from breaks

apart, and you remain alive,
is when you listen to the voice
of whom you mean to be...say, am I making
any sense at all? The night air,
maybe. Halloween. You have no choice,

although there seem to be so many. I've
a hunch you may be staking
quite a bit on that. Be fair,"

he warns, "to both of you." She stares
and almost asks, To whom? "It shows,
I guess." And Charley Morton waves
her on. Maybe I shouldn't try to block
it, she allows, and rubs her nose;
but how a man who says he cares
could act like that—she craves
a *close*. It's ten past by the Market clock.

Inside the Eucalyptus Bar, the noise
is vying with the smoke, is sighing
in the cozy air as people drink and eat
while, on the wall, a plaster gargoyle screams.
It's 8:15; poor Axel—who's been trying
far too long to keep his fragile poise
intact—shifts in his seat,
lips pursed. Only the gargoyle seems

to care, he notes, the fine old bar
filled as it always is with busy talk:
to all intents, an ordinary moment—yet. . . .

He turns a cautious eye to watch
for her appearance, stalk
her mood out while she's far
away enough not to have set
a front up, stirs his double Scotch,

and is about to take a sip
when Sweet Marie comes strolling in
and spots him instantly. He tries
to stand up straight but can't; her lips part;
and they freeze in place—as if a thin
hope neither will admit could somehow gyp
them, as it has before. Only their eyes
conspire to make a mockery of art,

reluctance hammering desire. She
sits beside him but she doesn't
take her coat off. "How—how are you?"
Axel asks. She answers, "Hi. I've got
a date at ten." Looks up. "This wasn't
easy, Axel." He replies, "I see, I see,"
shaking his head, mouth dry. "How far you
have to go. . .but, look—I'm not

prepared to say goodbye to you by ten.

Maybe by seven after." Eyes aflash,
she evenly replies, "What did you want
to say to me?" Her eyelid quivers too,
reminding him of how complete her brash
and tender spirit blazes, and of when
they last drank Scotch together, and the sky
was peach and blue and lavender and new.

He moves as if to speak. The waiter's come.
"I'll have the same," she says. He goes.
"Marie, I'm sorry for what happened. Look,
you have to understand. It's hard enough
to tell you what it is that—" "Heaven knows."
"Okay," he snaps in turn. "Why don't you hum
along? My God, you know—you know, you shook
me pretty bad. D'you have to act so tough?"

A shock, a tremor, sets her silky jaw.
"You bet I had to—Jesus Christ, you have no heart
at all," she screams, and starts to cry,
and doesn't try to care who sees
her. "Axel, what it once was, at the start—
I can't. I *can't* again. I'm just too raw
inside." She doesn't tell him how or why,
nor does his knowing help to ease

the silent weight that settles when her drink
arrives. She dabs her eyes. He cannot bear
to meet them, cannot speak. She looks out
at the smoky, varnished room. "You're bad for me,"
she says. He says, "I know. But, God, Marie, I care
so much for you, I didn't stop to think. . . ."
Again he shakes his head, mouth open, doubt
collapsing what he means to say or be;

she runs a finger down her glass and waits;
the chatter of the place breaks in again.
He rubs his eyes and says, "The only word
I feel with you is 'yes.'" She glances back
to catch a look so unexpected few men
ever show it, as it flickers and abates
like cooling embers that have just been stirred.
She gasps, and her resolve begins to crack,

suddenly seeing as certain women can
that what must burn must burn itself straight through
until it leaves no memory but of light
cascading. "Axel, I—" She cups his cheek.
"I didn't want to want this much from you."
Her wrist is smooth and cool. "No man
could understand that. But the fight

of it alone can make me weak
to the stomach, Axel. You're a guy.
Believe me, it's just not the same.
We love each other, or we fell in love—
and then what? Do you own me, say, next fall?"
He bites his lip. "Marie, I couldn't tame
you, couldn't trap you, and I wouldn't try.
It wouldn't keep you caring—and, besides, love
grows forever or it doesn't grow at all."

They finally leave at 1 a.m.
for her place, hoping to believe
in something slightly more than yesterday;
he shivers, catches breath,
as if by touching it to grieve
the hour its very chill. For them,
the cobalt darkness maybe whispers; they
are maybe not so terrified of death.

And how they'll manage, I don't know;
their answering machines
provide no useful clue,
their Amex cards no hint.
She's younger than she means
to be, although

she knows a thing or two,
has found her way by dint

of feeling near the edge
of everything she's not;
he's older than he'd like, the kind
of man who tries to learn to give
at moments when an awful lot
in him demands a hedge;
yet where the acid of the mind
has burned in them, the heart may truly live.

And air and moon
are absolutely still,
for once again
the witching hour prepares
to vanish, and the thrill
of knowing soon
how all will be when
each and every future dares

to be revealed
flies with it—out, away,
as if on pigeons' wings:
and who's to pity
this mysterious day
so arrogantly sealed,
or the fading midnight blue that sings
so thinly over the open city?

Ready or Not

You move
against me
like a startled thrush.

I feel
the blood beat reckless
in your cheek,

the message
of a trembling heart
along the wayward ridges

where our faces meet,
your sigh,
the hungry heat

of all of you
along my thigh,
leaning—

o my love,
I feel
each tremor

of the icy wind
against
your supple spine,

the living risk
of being
dangerously mine

uncertain
in your throat,
and why,

yet I
would hold
your breathless body close,

to still
the looming hour
a moment more

and have you stay,
one last dream
drifting by,

nestled

in the harbor

of my eye.

Sacre du Printemps

We come together
you and I
like swans

our feathers preened:
our supple lines
from neck to toe

are luscious
in the winter heat.
O Lord

the shivers
in my spine
swim round with you

and round
and round;
you make the ripples run

like sprays
of stars
across a narrow pond.

Sext

The pine is sixty feet
at least
and hangs head first
in the river,
water snuffling around it
the beige of a cantaloupe rind
(that rust and yeast
of death).

Yes, there are roots
as thick as arms
still clawing at the bank,
but one glance tells me
they will never last.
I sniff the breath of doom:
corpse in the river
of a wet spring
after a three-year drought.

And still the sky chatters,
hills folded on hills
adorn the light
that quenches me;
a new oak

strokes its forward branches
like bamboo
against the breeze,
hunkers down
not two feet from the fall-off,
has a chance
from even so impossible a perch—

but o the frost,
the first hard frost
after the next lean spring.

Tambourine

I hunger
for your arms,
your

mouth:
to sink
like grateful stone

into the deep
pelagic dark
of all you are,

the oldest
address
of your soul,

where even eyes
no longer
need to see.

I hunger for
the milky thighs
that whisper in my ear

of fire
and desert
dancing,

sand and silk
and tambourines
and flesh

no longer needing
any sound
to hear;

to touch
your skin
with weightless hands;

to lie
beside you,
still,

and feel
your breathing slide
on every nerve.

The Approach

O you moved
like smoke
the way you walked,

light
as a leopard's
tongue,

the air
you passed through
hurt to let you go.

It's true,
I thought,
arrested by

that steep incline
of eye,
that perfect mouth,

the tremor
in your
schoolgirl neck—

it's true:
a woman who
can be without

as she can be
within
is like the deepest pond

in open moonlight—
hush: like smoke.
You paused

and took
my breath away,
my *breath*

The Wave

Your being
was a wave,
and o

your melting mouth
the nestling surf
along my lips.

I felt
the deepest secret
of your tide,

the pull
of what
cannot be known

before a kiss,
a feeling
clear as stars,

as in
your slim hands'
supple spars

I rode
the rising wind,
and we

were so alone
together,
so adrift

This Poem Noise

This poem noise,
like the noise of a crowded room
or branch of birds,
must build its own sound:
plain facts
sharp as cracked glass.

Vespers

Off to the right,
two ladies guess
how high a hemlock
must have been

the year Bill
left for Yale—
ladies in pink
and blue, whose sins,

if any, never ran
to talking loudly;
and the shade,
like a bell at twilight,

spreads around them,
hushing the cars,
the clapboard white,
the river caught in flight.

We Knew Each Other
(for my mother)

We knew each other
as the turtles do.
No upstart creature Man
could tell us how to feel
the blood lean upward
with a keening moon

and when they aspirated her
(the cross-taped, inch-thick tube
shoved down her throat
like a stake), I knew
each syllable her eyes employed,
torn from a fern-dark language.

Now I'm stuck with words
when I yearn for nothing
but the silent patter of her feet
on the living room floor,
the touch of her cautious lips
on my unexpecting cheek.

West River Sundown

More doubt than mine
must haunt these ledges,
the gravel bank below
not where it used to be,
the beaver gone,
last year's uprooted oak
nearly a memory, and the mite
examining this notebook page
a bit of fauna I have never seen.

But the bullfrogs
are big, to judge
from the sound of them
across the spreading river,
and the blackbird's wings
are red as gold
in the light
as night descends
to call the evening truce.

So the beaver's someplace else,
and the bare-breasted girl
willowy as wheat

in her bikini bottom
and her baseball cap
who swam out toward it as I watched,
feeling my breath catch up
along the water flowing by her back.
Enough to know
I'll live less doubtful
than the black-eyed geese
coming in for the night
like C-5As from distant places.

*Live From
The Limelight*

Sex May Be Easy, But Passion Takes Class

Sex may be easy, but passion takes class:
Even if you've got a willing young lass
    with a hard little ass
    and her tits are like glass
and her mouth could turn brass into steam—
if you can't make her dream
that her heart is an orchid,
then, bubba, you ain't what you seem.

Sex is amazing, but love gets you high:
Even if you've got an eager young guy
    with a gleam in his eye
    and a bulge in his fly
and his sighs could make icicles burn—
if you can't make him yearn
to climb out of himself,
then, babe, you've got something to learn.

I am no one to talk, but I see all the clues:
You can do what you like to attract or amuse,
    you can hang out or cruise,
    you can be used or use,
but you must pay your dues to the heart—

if you can't be a part
of that deeper connection,
you'll never turn life into art.

AFTER THEY SHOT POOR JOHN WILKES BOOTH
(for Bob Smith)

After they shot poor John Wilkes Booth,
nobody came to claim him.
Nobody came to pay their respects
to his name

or bury the man. It was hard for Macmullen
to fathom;
at first, the mortician shrugged. He'd wait.
What fame

like that could do, he wasn't sure
(he'd seen the way
the sergeant who'd lost an eye on the ridge
at Antietam

spat on the ground where the body lay,
then marched his troop
past all the locals, sweat on their lips,
itching to talk,

to gulp a beer and tell again how the knees
gave out). But then,
"There's them that glory in another's shame,"
Macmullen told himself.

"There ought to be a bill paid out of that."
But days went by,

and no one showed, nor family nor friend.
The curious hung around

outside the shop like guards, to watch his sign
creak in the stifling breeze.
Even he didn't quite know what in the hell
would happen next.

The man would start to rot pretty soon, though,
and stopping it
would cost him more, in embalming lead alone—
but he was curious, too.

By morning, he made up his careful mind
and went to work.
When he was through, poor John Wilkes Booth
(what was left of him)

weighed six hundred pounds but would
no longer rot—
his whiskers, eyelids, finger scrapings, balls
all perfectly preserved

in oyster-colored lead. Washing up afterwards,
Macmullen even said
he thought he'd done a damned fine job.
A year sped by.

By then, his hopes of being paid were slim.
He'd pass the corpse

now and then in the course of his work.
One young assistant told him,

"It is...*eerie*, if you understand my meaning,
Sir," and had the strangest
shivering look in his eyes when he said it,
for that was *Booth*—

that eye, that hand, were "historic things,
Sir. Yes, indeed."
When nearly a year had come and gone,
Macmullen formed

a plan. Having by then a solid stake in Wilkes
(he felt
that even Mr. Lincoln would have recognized
his claim), and tired

of small town life (the curious no longer came,
nor the giggling
charmers who'd trail a white-gloved
finger down their necks

as they spoke), he dreaded dull routine,
the "inch by inch,"
and meant to do whatever he could about it,
he told the blacksmith

one fine day when the clouds were full of rain.
"Yes, sir. This May,"

Macmullen said. "That gives me time to put him
in a seat

and get the glass case made. I'll ship him
out, of course."
The blacksmith nodded. "Wha'd you say
he weighed?"

"A thousand pounds dead weight, I figure,
with the crate."
The blacksmith whistled. "Brace it good.
My Lord...hell,

if you charge a quarter of a dollar?
That'll bring 'em in."
"I surely hope so," said Macmullen. "Waited
long enough."

Such was the start of all that happened to him,
and to Booth.
By early fall, he'd made enough at the fairs
to pay the bill

and more. He'd seen a thousand faces look,
and saw they felt
exactly what the boy who worked for him had felt.
The following year,

he closed the undertaking parlor up for good
and took his trains,

meeting the freight at market towns and fairs,
draying out the crate

to set up in a tent that, as the years rolled on,
would need a patch
here and there
but prove quite sound, and raked it in—

a decent life for "old Macmullen," as they came
to call him.
He loved the lights, the girls who tittered,
even those

who asked him in a hush what Booth was really like,
their eyes trembling.
The sign read: SEE THE TRAITOR BOOTH,
WHO MURDERED MR. LINCOLN!

(That's the one he used up North. The other said:
JOHN WILKES
BOOTH—NEVER FORGOTTEN!)
Crossed Confederate flags beneath it

did the rest. Two decades later, old Macmullen died
one night,
asleep, in Omaha, and never got to meet
the freight next day.

Poor Booth, poor Booth, poor John Wilkes Booth—
Nobody came

to take away the crate. They finally sent it off
to *Unclaimed Mdse.*,

and there, amid the creaks of mice in a dark shed,
the century
rolled on and on, the railroad merged, was sold,
and sold again, and

then, in those heady robber baron days when piles
were being made,
a young man at a desk, just like Macmullen's boy,
forgot to list

that shed among Fixed Assets on a ledger sheet
for yet another sale.
The seasons passed, the country grew
and grew,

and poor Wilkes Booth sat frozen in the gloom.
What happens then
is anybody's guess. If there's a soul (a question
old Macmullen

never answered), maybe it begged release,
and maybe not:
I only know he sat there near a hundred years
of rain and sun,

a hundred years of country moving and moving,
until one Tuesday

in the early 1970s, when some young Wall Street
turk noticed

a number didn't tally on his print-out sheet
and checked.
A warehouse full of antiques, and the company
owned it? My.

They buried poor old John Wilkes Booth, at last,
in '71 or 2.
The foreman who uncrated him and saw those eyes
was munching

on a Burger King and fries. "Hey—get a load
of this!" he cried,
and all the guys came over. "Jesus Christ,"
one said. "Why, ain't he. . . ?"

Yes, he was, and let it be a warning, too—
although nobody dies
who tries to kill a president these days,
imagine what it's like

to hear the mice come scraping out at night,
to watch the flies
go circling round a hundred empty years,
the air that dries

a hundred years of moth wings drowned in rain,
and, all the same, you

realize that no one came, that *no* one *ever* came to claim you.

The Stars These Days

The stars these days have come and gone
with barely a passing nod from me.
I wonder if I'm scared to see
them, out there, always moving on.

A photo of a fossil leaf
captured my eye a day or two
ago. It was a head-on view
that nearly brought my heart to grief

of a fern that forty million years
had left their touch upon, and in
Antarctica no less. The cold,
dry hills that beckoned to my fears

had once been fat with stands of fern
swaying in sultry air. It seems
the fossil proves that reams and reams
of scholarship may have to turn

a new leaf over—this is how
marsupials made their fussy way
from South America, they say,

across a bridge to what is now

Australia, yet never reached
New Zealand. How the fossil tells
this all, what terrifying spells
were cast that sucked and squeezed and leached

whole continents, I can't conceive.
Enough to run my eye around it,
try to listen for the sound it
made in falling on that summer eve

before the ice age ground the earth
to frozen powder. Dare I hope
that my art twist as strong a rope
or witness half as fine a birth?

These College Girls

These college girls:
No man could fail to be reduced
by those thighs
to a thing that pants,
but for the eyes
that palpably deny his carnal myth;
and this
is his salvation.

Here are no harem curtains,
gauzy pink translucent silk
a hundred meters high—
only the lips that pause
on some uncertainty
that he has not anticipated,
so to suck
his marrow dry

in such exquisite pain...
not that he must not touch
the secret places all the boyfriends touch
(that part is easy),
but that, unreasonably

and without a single momentary care,
they love him. And for this
he draws his pay.

The Counterfeiter's Tale
(for Bob Smith)

Here's one I bet you never heard—about a guy
who sells real money
for forty cents on the dollar, and still makes
a profit. Honey

of a deal. It happened years ago. His name
was Ali, and
he had a knack for dreaming up amazing schemes,
for sleight of hand,

and for the patience only Egypt can instill
in someone—place
where time is taut and thin, and leaves
barely a trace.

Return with me to 1947. Finally, the war
is over, and life
in Alexandria is almost back to normal.
Sharp as a knife,

Ouldj Ali's lazy brain absorbs the news
that chatters

from his early morning paper. He's only wicked
when it matters,

like the time he suddenly vanished from the scene
of a scam he was working
on a certain Wehrmacht colonel, back in '41;
caught shirking

his responsibilities by turning Deutchmarks
into gold
on the sly, the colonel swore up and down
he'd been sold

a bill of goods, and easily could've
killed Ouldj Ali
when he failed to show up where he should've.
(What folly

to think that a man like that could be
so naive,
or trapped so easily. The General Staff
promptly relieved

the poor colonel.) Ali's been living his quiet
life ever since,

but funds are low—barely a quarter million left. A wince

escapes his upper lip. He sips his coffee,
studying the news.
Hardly a rustle under the awning in the square;
will he choose

to play his hand today, or still held off?
Orange gleams
the sun on the crest of the muezzin's tower.
Ali dreams

of quickly resuming the life he so enjoys—
a life of early
to rise, to nibble a bit of fruit and return
to his pearly

sheets (even alone, if he cares to); then,
a stroll along
the busy streets, a chat. . .he lights a Sobranie,
nods. It's strong,

the plan As judge of men, he hasn't
been wrong yet.

Rising, he pays his bill and enters the hotel;
though heavy-set,

he weaves like a feather through the cool, dim
marble space.
No one will ask him who he is, or what he wants—
he fits the place.

He calls a Cairo number from a booth.
"I have some bills,"
he says when his party answers. *"Hah?"*
The voice sends chills

up Ali's neck. "Dollars," he calmly says.
"Twenties. Good
ones. Send me a man on the train,
if you would. . . ?

Tomorrow morning? Fine. . . . Yes, yes!
the best I've seen."
Sure enough, next morning a courier comes.
He sees the green

is perfect on the counterfeit, the paper
masterfully made,

even the serial numbers're all consecutive.
"But you *know* we don't pay

more than a quarter on the dollar net,"
the courier declares.
"Then tell him this," says Ali— "on my sister's
virgin hairs,

for bills like these he pays me forty-five.
And tell him no,
I will not sell the plates. The plates I keep.
When you show

him these, I'm sure he'll understand."
Two days go by
before Ouldj Ali calls the man again. "And so?
You want to buy,"

he asks, "or not?" The frigid voice replies,
"How much you got?"
"Two hundred grand," our hero tells him, "just as
good as—*what?*

I told him *ninety* thousand net, my friend. . . .
Ah, well, all right then,

eighty-five it is, but not a penny less. . . .
Of course. . . . Tonight."

The afternoon grows silent, old; the market
empties, and the sun
begins to fade above the alleyways. He hears
the call to One

Whose Word is mighty, and he prays. So business
goes. At 10:00,
the train arrives. This time, an expert comes
and, when

he sees two hundred grand in twenties,
takes his time
examining the work while Ali waits contentedly.
There is no crime

in waiting; far beyond his window, stars are loud
against the hush
of endless sky. At last, the man looks up,
an eager flush

in his cheeks, and says, "*Yah, yah*. The best
I've seen in years.

You von't consider selling us the plates?"
Ouldj Ali sneers.

"For what? I couldn't ask enough. You'll make
out all right, too."
The other grunts and hands his satchel over.
"Peace to you,"

he says. Ali exchanges satchels, smiles,
replies, "And you.
Come, let us go together. Nights as cool
as this are few."

They make their way through lonely streets.
The Cairo man
says little. At the station, Ali murmurs,
"Safe trip, Stan."

"*Yah, yah.*" The expert boards and takes his seat.
After a while,
the train jerks slowly forward. But then, suddenly,
down his aisle

three gendarmes come, and the train shudders
to a dead stop.

They pass him by before one spots the satchel
sitting there on top

of the seat and barks out, "Is that yours?"
"Is—what?" Stan blurts.
"Oh. N-*no*. It was zere when I boarded. No."
And how it hurts

to keep his mouth shut as they take it, turn,
and leave the train.
Stan wipes his face. At least they didn't *get* him,
though the money's down the drain.

Yes, someone must have. . .but I wasn't
caught! he tells
himself again, and shakes his head.
The clock knells

12:00; the train regains its speed. Back on
the platform, Ali
watches it vanish quickly into night.
"Oh, my *golly!*"

he exclaims when the senior gendarme hands
his satchel back.

"You bring me so much joy, *effendi*, I cannot *say!*
There's such a stack

of *money* in there, you cannot imagine!"
The gendarme looks;
his eyebrows rise. "I swore to them
on the holy books,

effendi, on my sister's virgin lips, I swore
myself to see
this money was delivered safely. It is all,
all of her *dowry*,

effendi! I can't *repay* you for your diligence!
May Allah will—
but wait, I beg you—accept a mere gesture. . ."
he presses a bill

between the gendarme's fingers, and more, more.
"I beg you, *take!*"
He gives them each three hundred. It takes them
months to make

that much. The senior gendarme clears his throat.
"Better be

more careful in the future," he suggests,
tipping his cap. The three

stroll off, congratulate themselves in whispers,
take a peek
again at crisp, new, real American bills.
They barely speak.

Behind them, fixed in a stream of passengers,
Ouldj Ali smiles.
In his heart, there's a gull on the wing above
the souk. His trials

are over. He won't have to work again
for years. He brings
the satchel up against his linen-suited breast,
eyes closed, and sings.

Tisha B'av Follies

My summer camp was very Yiddish theater,
let us say: They liked to do it big.
We would be the band that followed Joshua
up to the walls—in the make-believe movie,
that is. We fought through color wars,
we played great ball, and boy, we had a theater
that could boast more seats than Off-Broadway.

We loved it, too. We once had Golda Meir
talk to us, when I was eight or so. She spoke
in the gazebo in the middle of the campus
where, as counselors, we carved our names,
and it was something then to mark a decade's tenure.
She told us all that pride was a thing like the sun.
That made good sense. Still does. It said

that to glow with warmth and daring was
to do it big. Anyway, the time this story
I want to tell you happened, I was working
as a senior counselor. Night of Tisha B'av,
we're marching campers down the road
to the lake. You have to understand—it's
full of mosquitos there at night, and the kids

are dressed in dark to mark the day.
Enter Division Leader right. "They're biting
already," I murmur. "Mm," he says, fiddling
with his lanyard, and heads on down ahead of us.
Out on the lake, the lifeguards have a raft.
Upon it, the Arts & Crafts department's built
the entire Second Temple in canvas and tempera.

The lifeguards watch the mike. Crickets
and flies and moths begin to surround us
as twilight falls. Then a voice explodes
from the P.A. system: *Tisha B'av!*
The words reverberate; the kids quiet down.
My children, it continues, we are gathered
to commemorate a day of bitter, bitter tears.

"Mikey, *stop* it!" one of my campers squeals.
"Stop talking," I growl. "But he pinched me."
"No I *din't*. He's got a *skito* bite."
Spot on Camp Director, upstage left, cloaked
in a coarse wool shawl. *And nights of bitter*
sorrow. See the Temple burning! See the fire
lick its way up, the stones turn black

with smoke. . .with smoke. . .turn black
with fire and smoke! . . . At last, the raft

is lit. The set begins to burn. *Children!*
the voice continues, and goes on and on and on,
building to a reverie of mourning,
an Oscar performance of grief. It's mosquitos twelve,
kids nothing, when the old trouper shrieks,

Let us weep for our brothers and sisters!
Let us moan for them! The next sound
that I hear is the wail of a wounded cow—
Aaaaauuuh! aaaauuuuhh! Let us raise
our voices up and moan! Oh no, I think:
he wants us all to do it! The kids start
laughing, scratching their legs as the show

goes on. But he *means* it, and soon he gets
us too to moan like a herd of disgruntled
sheep: *Aaauuuh, aaauuuuh, aaauuuuuuuuuhhh,*
the kids hysterical in all the noise keeping
the smiles from their faces like new recruits
as the bugs move in, the woods grow loud with stars,
and the temple burns its way down to the water.

But who am I to tear a memory down?
I drove up not too long ago to see the place again
before they turned it into summer condominiums.

The letters on the entrance sign were chipped
through seven layers of paint—an archeology
of more than boyhood, as vivid as the temple walls
that marked the smoking end of Joshua's road:

only a pregnant future breaking the sunlit silence.

Thin Air

The view is over rooftops—
looking west over rooftops that stretch away
tangled and unceasing
toward a far horizon
under shocked persimmon clouds.

It isn't hard to say
why such a sight should captivate me so.
It's not exactly what you call a pretty view,
not Paris *sur les toits*, not charming, God no;

it's a place where they use fake brick
and boxy greens to hide the scars of age,
where fourteen-year-old girls are steamy hot
and padded out to here by the time they're twenty,

a setting where the poor are uninspired
and none of the shopping carts at the A&P
runs straight. As such
the view is—how shall I say?—so pure,

for there is nothing in it to obstruct the pain.

The Pearl

Ah, Paris is a lovely town,
all travelers will agree—
and none more than a certain Count,
for reasons we shall see.

He went one day to Cartier's
with birthday-minded goals
(his worsted wools from Savile Row,
his car a chauffeured Rolls),

and asked to see a striking pearl
(the Countess loved them so.)
He took a glance at two or three
which weren't bad, but— no,

he wished to find "a special gift,"
he sighed emphatically,
caressing every syllable.
The clerk could plainly see

a major sale in the works and buzzed
to see the manager,
an elegant, alert, and busy
fellow, real tanager

of a man (burnt orange necktie setting off
his dark gray suit), but not
the least bit fussy regarding alarming sums,
or the least bit hot

for the sale—who rapidly appeared.
The Count was glancing at
a pearl-and-diamond pin. "*Monsieur
le Conte*, I gather that

you wished to see a pearl, something
unique?" Smiling, the Count
looked up. "Yes, something—*remarkable*.
It isn't the amount. . . ."

"*Mais oui*," the manager replied.
"I think I understand.
It happens that we currently
have just the thing in hand."

Indeed, it was a splendid pearl—
majestic, acorn-sized,
and of a pinkish-silver cast
particularly prized.

"*C'est magnifique!*" declared the Count,
and asked to have it sent,
writing a check for forty thou.
He wore a lovely scent,

the manager afterward recalled,
and used a gold-nibbed pen.
The pearl was hand-delivered to
an address in Enghien.

For quite some time, no more was heard,
'til the Count one day returned.
The manager bid a fond hello.
"You know, the Contessa has yearned

her whole life long for pearls," the Count
declared. "Tell me. The one
I bought—she wants an earring made
of it, and so. . .is there none

other like it? She would love the pair."
The dealer oozed regret.
"It was," he said, "a *rarity*."
"And you cannot get

another, if you try?" the Count,
crestfallen, asked him then.
"Perhaps. It may take quite
some time, of course—but when

we find it, I shall call *tout de suite*. . .
the price, you understand,
may be inflated—he who knows
we're searching tries

to charge accordingly." The Count
approved with a worldly shrug.
"Whatever it may cost!" he said.
"My darling has a bug

in her bonnet, the English would say."
The manager allowed
himself the barest smile,
and bowed

as well when the nobleman took his leave.
Two months went by before
their man in Africa replied.
He'd found a pearl—*peau d'or*,

extraordinary color, weight—
but eighty thousand francs
was rather high. The manager called
the Count, whose deepest thanks

were barely dampened when he learned
the price—a hundred thou.
"What does it matter!" he grandly said.
"For me, it is *a vow*

of deathless love!" The manager
assured him he would try
to call the instant it arrived,
and cabled his man to buy.

But when, in time, the pearl arrived
and Cartier's called, they found
the Count had vanished, totally,
and realized he'd wound

his web so well that he had sold
their own pearl back for twice
the price he paid. It wasn't fair
at all—but o so nice!

KID ON A BIKE

Back on a bike (10-speed, Hong Kong),
he claps his hand
once, twice,

glides by me, laughs out loud
once, twice, head back,
and the blade

of him slips through, blinks on and off
between the twilit trees.
A homely boy

(hair the best they can do for him,
eyes too small and angled down,
wears braces),

timid boy—but oh, the explosion
of hands as they clap
once, twice,

(Like *alright! Do* it!), laughing hands,
a massive screw propeller
driving, driving

Christ Church Cemetery, Philadelphia

What close to thirty decades had in store
Clings like a stormy cloud bank to the stone.
The oldest graves are marked by nothing more.

When freezing rain had chiseled to the core,
Obliterating words, and left as bone
What close to thirty decades had in store,

The silence was the kind that follows war:
Because all final rest is rest alone,
The oldest graves are marked by nothing more.

And though I yearn to know what came before—
The terror it must once have been to own
What close to thirty decades had in store

For those lost names on that inchoate shore
Who might have guessed, or feared, or even known
The oldest graves are marked by nothing more—

Death, in whose syntax only nouns restore
The breath of memory, has merely shown
What close to thirty decades had in store:
The oldest graves are marked by nothing more.

Raining

Is it raining or not this afternoon,
the gray air soft but sharp?
Unless I get up, go and have a look,
I swear I just can't tell.

Whether the window's not quite clean
or my eye's too tired
(been editing all day—stuff like
a British firm recently came out with
something called a "smart brassiere"
that monitors your temperature
to see if you're pregnant—
item in a book
on technological overload)....

It isn't raining yet.
I rub my eyes and stretch my arms
and wonder
how this life,
small garden patch,
this working out
of one man's piddling choices
will appear in fifty years

(who cares to know?
who even thinks to ask?)—

will any of it fly?
Will anybody out there,
me included, think I should
have sat here, in this chair,
causing the rain to fall?

No Luck at All
(In Memoriam L.D.)

I

Long afterward another autumn's bleeding out
and I'm still wondering
what it is precisely I've lost
since you patted my hand in thanks
as I drove you to the hospital
and I shrugged it off as if to say
it's nothing
nothing really
the least I can do

He'd called two hours before
asked me to come
said it was bad
that you wouldn't leave the apartment
but maybe if I came and talked to you

There was *Hawaii Five-O* on the tube
and we watched it
I mean maybe you watched it
I faced it
waiting for the words to come to me

stealing glimpses of the wreck the place was in

When he went to the john
you cast a sidelong glance my way
lips poised above the glaucous rim
of a vodka snifter
your eye the winter steel
that lurks in a fish hawk's stare
and said
I think it's the liver bladder kidneys
all of it

You got to let them help you
I said
Your hand trembled
nearly lost the cigarette
Nyaah! you grunted

It was
an inside joke my dear
it came to little more

I kidded you that I was kidding you
you kidded me that you believed it too
going through the motions

getting dressed
pulling a dirty brush
through hair so lank and tired
the light had long since flown

it was
the only way
to die a civil death

2

I knew you
when a feather
could have broken down your breath

and every moment
was an act of faith
in the triumph of touch over pain

You were crying
face down on your bed
the windows black with summer rain

I patted your back
What did I know

Never been really drunk a day in my life

Here be dragons
Protestants and holy ghosts
Here lie the sharpest edges of the perfect knife

I should be made
of harder cloth
be robed in plain gray speechless wool

and sit with hands
bunched stiffly in my lap
Forgive me for the load I cannot pull

3

Taste our blood
o my dear
speed your soul
to gather near

Wrap the river
round your leaving
as a sacrament
receiving

See my hands
in motions making
stars descend
and daylight breaking

And in silken
candle shadow
see the light
escape this meadow

Touch the tendril
to the bark
for ours is all this
cruel stark

upheaval
grating glitter
bursting star
and bar room titter

bursting star
and bar room titter

Spring Cleaning

I'm cleaning off my desk today
when I find a Visa bill
sandwiched accidentally
between a tax rebate complaint
and my canceled checks from a month ago

and you know how that makes you feel:
at first, *Oh shit, it's late,*
I'm gonna pay a penalty,
they'll take away the card,
they'll burn my food,
they'll shoot me in the knees;

and then, *Oh, fuck! The damn account*
is barely balanced now.
I'll bounce this one to boot.
They'll charge me sixty-seven bucks for that
before they're through—
I'll got to jail for kiting checks.
I'll die in jail, I'll die in jail.

Except the bill says
(when I get the nerve to read it)
"Minimum Payment: $0.00"...
Tell me—do you laugh or cry?

Come Again?
(*for Don Kmetz*)

I

Some years ago I was standing
in the parking lot
of a suburban restaurant
while a minister I knew
confessed to me again and again
in a tortured whisper
that he liked fucking
boys. He'd somehow
got it into his head
that I would be
the perfect person
to absolve him.

His look was riveted
in shame to the ground
as he spoke to me,
and I could not stop my gaze
from drifting to a corner of the lot
where I'd been parked
one frigid night a month before
with the wife of a guy I knew,

a woman with huge gray eyes
and the gorgeous face
of a bruised *chanteuse*,
who managed to straddle me
against the driver's wheel.
Our breaths were mingled steam.
I came too quick,
and she murmured,
"I figured," and sighed. . . .
So I absolved the minister,
felt very good about it, too,
our wayward lives conjoined within
the constellation of the place.

2

I'm feeling the same just now
on this Chelsea street
where I often walked
in another life.
It's summer, and the smell of box,
the Hopper-colored buildings,
flowers in window boxes,
birds, the angles and the curves,
are wiping out a decade,

maybe more.

Faces I could photograph
stare up from corner stoops;
bodies caught in touching postures
reach for a plum
or clean out a drain.
I was hot then, too,
to get laid,
though my body's only clear recall
is of an endless tightening
around the temples
and the strain
of too much on the mind,
too little in the pocket.

I take a seat on one of the stoops
on the shady side of the street,
and it is only after I have stared
at the roofline
of the brownstone just across from me
burning red and blue in the sunlight
that I recall
the con man who was sitting here
as I passed

who spent a good ten minutes
trying to explain
why he needed twenty dollars,
refusing—actually refusing
to believe I didn't have a twenty.
Though I did,
I finally convinced him otherwise.
He was a pretty good con man,
but I,
after all, was a poet.

3

Is it clear at all,
what I'm saying?
I've spent a lifetime
filtering this slag
through any medium at hand,
trying to make a little sense
of what I can recall,

and now
that I can segregate at last
the asinine,
the tempting,

funny, sad,

the singularly dear,

I find

to my dismay

it was the *way* they touched,

the crease they left upon each other

as they lay in folds,

that counted—

only that

which sent the jolt of passion through

and made them

stay alive.

Confession
(for Eugenia)

One of these days, my love,
I'll wake up knowing
I don't have the time left
for the things I always said
I want to do—take a camera
into the hills
when dawn first stuns the blue hour,
swim to a reef
that quivers purple in a green lagoon,
behold the legends hang like ice
from cliffs in Katmandu.

One of these days, yeah, maybe—
but for now I'd just as soon
cast off, bare-poled,
into the endless moonlight of your eyes;
as soon curl up like this,
my head in the crook of your arm,
my cheek against your breast,
the cats like fallen apples
at our feet.

*Email: Poems
In Real Time*

BRIGHTER NOW
(for Ed Hack)

I mostly think of you
on flat white winter days like this
that cast no shadows
but that make me wince
as if to ease a pain
wedged in beneath my eyebrows

I see you puzzled in the yard
hefting a broken implement you've found
One further evidence
of life's unending failure to endure
Your lips are slightly parted as you plan
how next to regulate the universe

I'm there beside you
sucking on a tooth
and we've been doing that so long
I can't remember when we ever didn't
People things or words
the way you lift them
when they've broken down
collapse or fail to fire
speaks volumes of intention to my ear

The stubble on our cheeks is brighter now
than any other feature of our faces
Winter lingers longer in our eyes
and when we fail to start a conversation
perhaps it is because
we've drained the subject of surprise
and can't be kidded into thinking otherwise

although it may just be we've learned at last
to speak the silent dialect of love
one instant at a time

And so
improbably
we have survived
Daily the smell of soap reminds us

Hot to Trot

How much of your life
do you figure
have you spent
on calculating the effect
your looks produce in men

And how much has been spent
by others who react
to the envies
that flicker in your eyes
as if in heavy honey
searching always *always*
for a way out
of here
a way to strike for *there*

No wonder
you look so ripe
so fuckable
How very much mistaken looks can be

A Pal
(for Linda Principe)

It is so fine
to look into your eyes
and know the caution there
is not for me

Oh yes you feed upon yourself
and I am like another you
but you and I
have nothing left to hide

We neither joust nor mate
but reach two fingers
side by side
into the same air   plum   pursuit

same firmament
God bless this singularity
If you had balls you'd be a pain
And if I didn't who knows where we'd be

Passing in the Hall
(for Marina del Risco)

When I look into your eyes
I have to translate into Spanish
ask How private is this moment
meant to be

As I was doing the wash
in the laundry room today
I read the Board was planning
to buy you a maid's cart

and I was pained to think
you might have felt the shame of it
across your cheek
It stuck in me

until I asked myself
how do you call yourself
when you're not dreaming
what words define your work

a woman who has sued a man
for child support

and won her case

although she's living with him

Pedal to the Metal

Women or trucks
you ride 'em hard
you jam the gears
and when they break
you get annoyed

How come you never learned
to breathe

Was it your dad
who beat it out of you
Or your mom
who kept cutting peppers
in the kitchen

The thing of it is
you could live to be a hundred
and never escape
never be different
if you don't blink

From the Poetry License Bureau
(for Adele Schwartz)

At the end of every rainbow

lies a wreckage or a poem

and you've made your move

Let the sons of bitches take away

whatever they can find of you

The residue they leave behind

(the stuff they'd never see

because it glitters

like the ghosts of ice in melt water

like air on a mirror)

will be yours and tomorrow's

Not that it will help

put food in your mouth today

No no the Fates do not find

poetry amusing

Plat du Jour
(for Susan Summerbell Chval)

We meet for lunches
where all the corporate bunches
hang out around here
(horsy women with too much hair
men who're barely there)
places with plenty of cheer

We nibble spaghetti
debating the petty
miseries of life
content in this familiarity
this distillate of how to be
without conceit or strife

Uncivil indeed to suggest
that in this state we test
what would happen if
I said I thought your husband stays
a bit remote or you found ways
to hint I sometimes bore you stiff

You know such moments won't arise

Unlike some other gals and guys
we've given up the need
to score a cheap point or to flush
out the hard light that falls like a hush
on everybody's sourest deed

Leave that to others
If I had my druthers
I'd only want to take my camera and my wife
up an alpine meadow stream
I know and live the kind of dream
they have to cut you loose from with a knife

Soon You Will Forget Your Own Name
(for Dan Balaban)

Soon you will forget your own name
You will wake up one morning
and in place of who you are
you will find a yawning blank

Seized by images of shrunken genes
and spindly ganglionic threads
you will shrink in horror
cursing all the lousy water you've consumed

the cigarettes and dope and coke
pastrami butter store-bought mayonnaise
bad air in congested tunnels
poor bowel movements

Do not be distressed
It will not be a stroke that does you in
or the start of some Alzheimer process
but the latest positioning of Microsoft

Bill Gates will smile at you that day
and wink in his demonic faintly walleyed way

selling you updated software of yourself

over which he holds monopolies of trade

Lately the Sunlight on Your Face

Lately the sunlight on your face
has been revealing flat plateaus
that used to be rolling hills
Age finally shows itself
in ways like that
We bellyache about crow's feet
about lines that radiate out
from the corners of the mouth
These are not signs of age
they're billboards

But that flattening I see in you
like a thinner slice of bread
so saddens me I lose my place
Where once a brook barked frantically
around a fallen log
a claw now whips
and the spray of water on my sweater
has become a spatter line of blood

You Get My Business Card
(for Annamarie Amodio)

You get my business card
you got my address phone
my fax my email number
and in not too long my web page site as well

I feel like I'm a point in space
triangulated constantly by satellite
in instant real-time touch
with all tomorrows

But hush
You one of those
who thinks those things are nice
for those who need them

but you don't
(the way some used to say
No no I don't smoke pot
Get high on life instead)

as if these numbers are some kind of crutch
Or maybe your deep-downest snapshot

of yourself is of a barefoot gardener
straw hat bucket of chicken shit in hand

and you like making electricity
the old-fashioned way
All I can say is Do not kid yourself
Email is not a fad though faddists hang around

and it's not a con
though fortunes inconceivable
have been and will be made from it
We're being reinvented

by the mouse click on an icon
opening to worlds beyond our ken
and if you fail to see the contrail
of that flaming arc

the air you breathe will be an older air

So Here's What I Tell Her
(for David at 30)

Friend of mine confesses
she'd have jumped my bones
25 years ago or so
if she'd just had the nerve

Her husband's so uptight
The sex between them's never been too good
He only says I love you
if she says so first

She tells me this
because she knows (she says)
that I'm a happily married man
and there's no risk

So I'm speechless Right?
And then she wants to know
how is it I have
such good relations with my kids

I want to say
Oh God I caught a break there

But will she understand
if I let on

that you were with me in St. Croix
the night I gave up smoking dope
because my thigh began to twitch
all by itself and you said

Shit Pops what the hell is that?
And will she get it
if I tell her
that I worry all the time about you

but I rarely say a word if I can help it
any more than I do with friends
because I don't think that it shows respect
to treat your children any differently?

Better to bitch about my own luck
when I'm broke and the sleet's
dripping down my miserable back
(or crab about whether I can get it up today

or whether I can keep my head in place
or act a bit less like the fool I am)

than interfere with other people's lives
So here's what I tell her

Love's like watering a plant I say
You pour and pour
The water gurgles down and disappears
A day or two it's like you never watered it

and that's the story But the leaves still grow
And do they owe the water anything at all
because it flows Or you because you pour?
And isn't that the kind of love she's missing?

Over and Over and Over
(for Susan Balaban)

For some a tree's a tree
and giddy leaves in spring
for others more a hand
upraised before the mooring sun

But there are those like us
who see instead
an upward thrust of green
whose daily pain is bark

I've had my fill of lucid curves
I want the glassy edge of life
the stuff that neither dries out
nor dissolves like bone or rock

I want sheer motion   endless   upward
rolling over on itself like wheat
(yes yes the curl your tongue just made
the turning twist   the energy of that)

FAT KID
(for Eugenia)

Going to buy croissants
for your birthday breakfast
I pass the fat kid on the street
He's got his tiny dark eyes fixed
on the ground in front of him
thinking hard it looks like

working his way through something
And I make like I'm gonna wave
but think better of it
Who knows what I'll interrupt
He's still about three-fifty maybe
five foot six like me

and has that sweet cherubic face
all round and red
and button Irish
First time we ever spoke
at five a.m. one bitter winter day
in the elevator

he was almost done

delivering the papers
and I was on my way to teach a class
Delivering the papers
early in the morning
and working as a crossing guard

are what he does He sweats a lot
year round Hey how ya doin? I asked
Oh pretty good he said
big smile white teeth those eyes
all crinkled up It's just the details
though They get to me

The details? I replied
Yeah details Like if someone cancels
Stuff like that he said
keepin track of stuff
But hey though whatcha gonna do?
I nodded Whatcha gonna do

So now I turn and watch him
rumble past me eyes compressed to beads
He settles on the upturned
plastic carton that he uses
when he wears his orange vest

and keeps an eye on all those children

going by On all that laughter kidding
nudging-elbows kid stuff
Kids who never even see him there
who never track him on their way
He's sitting there but now it's summer See?
School's out There's no more kids at all

Dress Boy
(for Jack Camhe)

Eight in the morning in walks Dave
thin as a rail horse face a pencil moustache
chocolate Borsalino at a rakish tilt
two shades darker than the collar
of his Chesterfield pigeons cooing
on the window ledge
The racket of the cutting tables
on the floors below won't start till nine

Hey kid he growls I brought a bagel
How's it goin Dave?
You know The way it does he says
He draws the panatela from his mouth
and stares a moment at the ash
He nods he disappears into the loft
and comes back minutes later with a smile
You need a dozen 12s and four 16s he says

You know That number with the bugle beads?
I nod I'll send them up he says
Okay I say We eat the poppy bagel
with a cup of coffee Pigeons

break the silence while he puffs away
rolling the thin cigar in a cared-for hand
I finally say You mind
I ask you something Dave?

A course not kid he answers
narrow face in profile still
sad-sack eyes turned toward me What?
About the forty-three ten
Oh he chuckles *That*
I take a sip of coffee and I say
You know the market's talking
Sure it is The market always talks

So whatcha want to know?
(Okay, so here's what happened
Dave was cutting Christmas goods in crepe
and this one model 4310 scoop-neck A-line
with these bell sleeves in a heavy lace
just started walkin off the racks
nine weeks ago We're talkin *life*
the way the lace drapes on the hanger

Really buys the look He's selling it
for 59 You figure

he's got what three weeks before the knock-offs
hit the street and then it goes to 40
and 30 20 10? But somehow *somehow*
when the boys from Spiegel's try to find the lace
they can't
Supplier's got this whatchacall "computer"

running inventory in some Carolina warehouse
Who the hell knows what The goods are
Uh they say "misplaced" Computers
Something So four weeks go by and five
and six and now it's nine and everybody knows
the man has made the killing of the year
A mid-price party house Unheard-of luck)
So here you are I tell him Sitting here with me

the same as always Yeah he says
He's finishing the bagel Well I say
It ain't my business but you musta made
a pile of gelt by now Dave
Ohh yeah he says a slow grin breaking up
his narrow mouth the pencil moustache too
Oh you might say He leans in close his eyes are big
Between us kid I put away *four mil. net net* so far

Well Dave I say I just can't figure it
I mean if it was me I wouldn't be here
sittin with a bagel I'd be sittin
I don't know in Malibu or someplace
Then kiss the girls for me he says
with an out-loud laugh and sighs and adds
Now listen kid I like you. Come in early every day
it shows you're serious A dress boy though you ain't

The old sad eyes meet mine and go right through me
Kid the market gives the market takes away
That ain't the point at all
I make it big today So what? Tomorrow
all of it could fly away It has before
It will again But if I lose it all
tomorrow or the next day or the next
I'll get right up put on my spit-shined shoes

my brown suit with the sharp-pressed crease
my Chesterfield my yellow gloves
my Borsalino at the perfect angle
and I'll walk right down the center of that street
just like I owned it That's a dress boy kid
He pats my cheek and rising adds *Enjoy* this life

Not to Put Too Fine a Point on It
(For the dead, September 11, 2001)

I

Reaching 42nd
from the ferry stop at 38th
after a sunset crossing
air as crisp and dry
as Taos light
river the blue and black and white
of a Ruoault waterscape

we passed a cop car
angle-parked
in front of a precinct house
and cordoned off
with yellow crime-scene tape
no windshield left in back
but a bashed-out hole
and covered by an inch or more
in gray cement dust

On the back seat
papers and a Mars bar wrapper
sat as if composed forever

in a snapshot
buried halfway under
another drift of dust
my first untelevized encounter
with this death

Here is my mouth
it said
my open mouth
come to devour
to tear you limb from limb

Next day we went back
in that bright honey orange
sunset glow
holding each other more for comfort
than against the chill

as a black guy with biceps
the size of my thigh
came strolling by
in a baseball cap
sunglasses
dark blue tee
read FEDERAL AGENT on the back

a 15-round Beretta on his belt
a spare clip too
neat leather case
no way to lose it accidentally
This was no minimum wage guy
working airport check-in
This was a guy knew how to move
brain like a razor

2

Look down the river
you can see the smoke
weeks later

Bodies says a friend
That's bodies too
not just a building
People burn their dead
in plenty places
all across the world
they always have
my wife points out
Oh yeah I tell her
Nazis too

We have registered by now
the near escapes
the friends of friends
who didn't make it
all the stories
piled on edge against each other
like twisted beams
or body parts

We know
that we're depressed
because we wake up
in the middle of the night
four o'clock or thereabouts
and can't go back to sleep

We tell ourselves
that we'll pick up
where we left off
and life goes on
go back to work
eat out
have conversations
but (not to put
too fine a point on it)

my heart has stopped a splinter
of the glass
came off that cop car
yes

and it will grow new skin
to cover
but the shard
won't come out

3

Look   Don't string me up
if I make mention
(not to put too
fine a point on it)
that hunger breeds an open mouth

I wish that I could
slowly peel the skin
off those who murdered here
but none of that will clothe
the wretched

Recently Mercedes Benz

released a car for sale
"street version" of a racing model
goes from zero to sixty
in five seconds flat

hand-made
worth the wait
the ad read
and I wonder if they'll sell well
in Kabul Damascus or Beirut

or how about Louis Vuitton
or golden kiwi
Montecristo smokes
Italian tuna packed in glass

at just eight bucks
for seven ounces

4

Another friend describes a conversation
with a New York fireman
how the guy said
ten days into the rescue effort

at Ground Zero
he had finally found
his first whole object
Office stapler
Barely recognized it
for a moment

having spent ten days
sifting only
through pieces of rubble
the size of thumbnails
Pieces of walls and bodies

5

The thing is
What will we *yearn* for now
who hard-assed
sun-glassed
claim we've seen it all
been there done that
heard all the hard-luck stories
all the inside jokes
that we've been worked by pros
and yet can tell

the genuine authentic article
at forty feet
No way
Instead
I feel as soft as milk
and unprepared
for the stomach clench of childhood
all over
again
Mommy, Jimmy hit me
hit me hit me

and not to put too fine
a point on it
the kite I let go of
the kite that was dancing
in the lucid orange light
has vanished
What will we dream of now
when we dream of building
castles to the heart
in the sky

You fit it all together

Pasadena Blonde
(to Stacey Thomopoulos)

I

In a café in Berkeley
where they'll give you soy milk
with your latte
for just a half a buck more

I am nursing an espresso
with a dash of milk and score
as my wife murmurs reasonably
to my son about engagement rings

She's better at these things than I
though she is not his mother
and even if the boy and I
are like two fingers on a peace sign

People sit around us
with the layered Berkeley look
hair where you least expect it
like the light

which now is apricot Tequila sunrise
clinging close to everything
The place stands on a corner
Out the plate glass window

men and women glide along on bikes
and talk and walk and think
And then I spot
the corner street sign

Channing and Shattuck
I mouth the words My mind goes blank
goes curling through a warp
of almost forty years

2

Amy she said
I said Is this your seat
Oh no she said It's just you're kinda cute
Nobody'd ever said a thing like that to me

nice Jewish kid from City College
She was in shorts and uniformly gold
(except her gray eyes and white teeth)

Hi Amy Um I said She sat beside me

Course was Intro to the Pastoral
You must be grad she said
as others ambled in
(five hundred seats An amphitheater)

Yeah I am I said You undergrad?
I asked as if it wasn't obvious
She nodded eagerly and pointed
to the syllabus

D'ja ever hear of these guys?
Luminous the eyes
Her voice already a conspiracy of two
Um yeah I said A few

What was it two days later
Amy asked if I could stop by her place
down on Channing talk about the Eclogues
Sure I said and showed up two two-thirty

Hi she waved Come on in
She was finishing a sandwich
(Velveeta cheese on white bread)

turned and kissed me hard

We didn't get to Virgil
didn't get to anything
but naked flesh until the sun went down
That girl was everything I'd ever dreamed

of California everything the smell
of eucalyptus hinted at
So taut so sure so happy to be willing
I could hardly dream I was awake

And then the sunlight
fading to rust the wind
a quiver in the curtain by her window
her tongue a memory on my chest

she rose like dawn from my embrace
leaving me breathless watching every step
and grabbed the sandwich
Three more bites and it was gone

and Amy too to what was coming next
She was the best a guy could find
although I couldn't picture holding her again

nor would it have dawned on her to try

3

I drift back to the talk
the coffee smells and hisses
Nothing's been resolved
but things are clearer

through no agency of mine
Sooner or later he will take
the step toward this I have
That's clear to me

The rest is atmospheric
like our needy lives
a hint of cloud or light
the memory of something bright

and all the rest
will take care of itself
So Amy taught me
half a block up Channing worlds away

What He Never Told Me
(For George Koukounas, Ob. March 6, 2002)

I

Captain shuffled over to me
one day after dinner
with the local paper in his hand
local for him that is
Greek paper from Kardamyla

pointed in the obits
to a face
(framed in black)
cleared his throat
fiddled with his glasses

said *He was a captain*
paused and added
He made two dowries
Brought his family to Argentina
Never had one accident

I waited to hear more
until the captain shuffled off
and I realized that's all there'd be

One whole life scrubbed down tight
to sixteen words

enough to signal through the fog
enough to chisel on a rock
That's what you call a man
of few words
Mourn him too now

gone on his final voyage
pack of cigarettes again in hand
coffee with five sugars in the cup
covered by a napkin keep the flies away
Sit there on the bridge and mourn him too

2

Where he came from
there were no fathers

gone to sea they had
to earn their sisters' dowries

There was nothing else to do
but pray and farm

And so grew up
a town without fathers

for so many hundred years
as hard as rock

where boys went out to earn
and mothers ran the family

I could see in his deep eyes
this having had no father

in his daily life Mine died young
when I was twenty-three

so I could tell
No wonder the man was inward

not so much a keeper of secrets
as a spar adrift

No wonder it bred thick sinew both
and sentimental eyes

baked dry by sun and wind

No wonder life was funny for him

who could see it sparkle
with the faith of butterflies

yet so chock full of fools
clinging like crabs to earth

or gold
(which sinks the fastest)

there were few words left
to cover

3

Give him what he wants
Dear Lord
He was his solitary self
and we can ask no more

The shogun of Japan
once caused a plaque
to hang around
the neck of Basho

as he aged
that read
(for anyone who kept
an inn or tavern anywhere)

Give him what he wants
and send the bill to me
They say the poet drowned
drunk in a pond

a few years later
happily I'm sure
The captain would have laughed
at that He knew

Hot Shiskebab
(for Jim Dette)

I

Hot shiskebab hot pretzels
shouts the vendor
advertising strictly halal meats

square guy a round dark face
a two days' growth of beard
a brush moustache

I order a stick of chicken
hand him a ten
He throws the chicken on We wait

Three girls come by
Hot shiskebab hot pretzels
hot boyfriend he shouts

They keep on walking
and he sighs
He offers me a knowing wink

Hot shiskebab he shouts again
hot pretzels
hot boyfriend

studying their pert behinds
the way they walk
indifferent laziness

Just two guys on the street
my people maybe murdering his
this very minute in the Gaza Strip

two guys who maybe would've
raped those girls for kicks some centuries past
and blamed them for it too

He says She needs Can see
You don't say
Oh yeah yeah She needs hot boyfriend

I can tell He asks me do I want
hot sauce or barbecue
or special lemon sauce

I say No Leave it dry
And no bread either

as he eyes the blonde

now disappearing down the street
She needs one Yeah
He almost keeps my change

2

All this is happening a block away
from a lie-in blocking Broadway
and 40th to oppose the war

in Iraq
Just hours ago
there was no protest

Going to the Small Press Fair
a couple blocks away I didn't see a soul
but now the noise is sheer as steel

the cops have blocked off
half the streets
They're wearing riot gear

tac helmets manning all the corners

under signs for Claiborne Pepsi
Disney It's the New Broadway

a Ginza for us round-eyes
full of naked midriffs tits and dollar signs
the tourist windrows all agog

It's all hot shishkebob
hot pretzels
and an oh so steamy boyfriend

What We Were Talking About
(for John Melis)

What we were talking about
the other night over dinner
sticks in my hand
like a sliver of glass

Not so much the point
you were trying to make
or the tedious parry I insisted on
that neither of us cared about

as the sense of time frozen in place
Your table was so pleasant
course after course
the air so scented with ease

I had a chance for once
to touch the inside of your skin
and was surprised
how rough it was

You went on after I'd
stopped caring

what we were talking about
went on and on

like a boy
so happy to have killed a bug
you wanted to kill again
and I was afraid

you'd notice
that I wasn't listening
before you called a truce
wasn't listening at all

but rubbing
my thumb and forefinger
over the callous
on the inside of your skin

The Girl in the Low-Cut Jeans
(for Susan Rocco)

The girl in the low-cut jeans
cropped tank top
tight tanned midriff
hair tied back in a low gather
has such an ass

But she's standing
at the corner
in the pouring rain
with a look on her face
that hints

she may have hit the wall
that stops a pretty girl
the wall that says Guess what
It doesn't work
the way you thought

My windshield wiper's
working hard
to smear her chiseled looks
uncertain bottom lip

and nervous shoulders

into fingerpaint
I'm waiting for the light
She's waiting for God knows what
She has the light
Her hair is getting soaked

Sometime or Other
(*for Jason Balaban*)

Sometime or other
we'll all get past the stench
of body counts

the plain obscenity
of telling folks our glory's
worth a few dead soldiers

blown up in a convoy
like so many armored
sitting ducks

Those boys won't see the glory
None of them will see
their two-year-old

declare herself herself
the fading violets
of autumn skies this year

or who wins next season's
Oscar No the dead hear nothing

but the wind of maya

Listen carefully
and you can hear it too
It makes a hiss

like water going down a fall
like air escaping from a tire
like the sharp death rattle

none of our brave
flag-toting leaders
ever heard

When I Miss You
(for Eugenia)

When I miss you
it's not like
it once was

aching pain
that haunted me
at night

It's worse
I miss you now
beyond a sense of me

We are a tree
together
and the trunk

has just been split
by lightning
 straight down the middle

Missing you now
is not a thing

but a vacant space

from which
no sound or light
escapes

Walking Man
(for Gordon Rapp)

Guy could be a hiker
tanned arms hunter tee shirt
canvas pants dark shades
in brilliant morning light
on a hillside road
overlooking the river

but where you'd see the backpack
there's a carry cart instead
the square wire kind
old ladies wheel
their stuff home in
from the supermarket

This one's jammed to the top
with swollen plastic bags
containing his whole life
that homeless sign
I cannot help but think
And why? I ask

It makes no sense

and yet the eyes
do not deceive
The eyes are like
a photograph
as much as is

the other way around
You may have seen the ones
I'm thinking of
The first the one from 1839
guy in a top hat
one foot resting on a stoop

looking away from the camera
or the one that Capra shot
of the Spaniard's hands flung out
falling backward in slo-mo
rifle slipping from his grip
at the moment of death

Life is pictures Yes?
Like these? Like this
walking man seated
on a public bench
and fiddling

with his complex hive of bags

Candid images
that so disrupt the pace
of calendar and watch
Palm Pilot Post-It note
our muscular belief in Doing
just so we can say it's done

before we are
At least he's in the sunlight
More than I can say for me
At least he walks a lot
He must How else could he
have gotten such a tan?

Let Me Suggest the Following

Now that you've discovered
your solution to the problems you confront
will not work

a number of choices
are available to you
One You can deny they will not work

as you have for most of your life
which is fine if you think
you will live forever

Two You can try doing just the opposite
because you think deep down
that that's the way the world works

I have seen marriages constructed
on just such flimsy assumptions
You don't want to know how they ended

Or Three you can listen to me
in which case
since I finally have your attention

let me suggest the following
since I had to take the same advice once
and it didn't kill me

though the welts took time to heal
Stop just stop
There's nothing easier

though little we are less inclined to do
It is as if
surrounded by dark-fanged demons

about to seize you
by the neck
and seeing there is no way out

you wake up with a deep gasp
from a dream and think
God just imagine if it was really happening

TANKA
(for Eugenia)

Darkness The cat sleeps
head on your lavender tee
the edge of my hand
on your unused pillow
Momentary peace for two

Two Haiku
(for Roy Lucianna)

1

For you adrift in
fog I light this smokeless stick
The scent is close by

2

Breeze after nightfall
Heart opens to another
Then come endless stars

I Want to Thank

I want to thank
whoever found my gloves
in a shopping cart
at the supermarket
and dropped them off
at Courtesy

You probably will not
remember them
Plain black men's leather gloves
And what you did
it wasn't anything
the Catholics make you a saint for
Believe me I know
I've done the same

But I was running on empty
when I lost them
my business on the ropes
my latest novel still unsold
and in complete despair
They call it mild depression
And you renewed my faith

It wasn't much

but it was everything

I Keep on Writing Poems
(for Eugenia)

I keep on writing poems so the sound
can intercept the silences that fill
the room when you are gone And still and *still*
I can't convince myself that you're around
I manage best to manage if I've found
some trace of you (receipt or long-paid bill
you didn't plan to throw away until
I saw it) Otherwise I come unwound

The empty spaces in my lonely art
spread out around me like a rippling pool
Resisting though I try I sink and start
to drown *Then* only I recall the cool
touch of your fingers on my breathless heart
and I no longer feel like such a fool

How Many Times
(for my daughter)

Can't begin to tell you
how many times
I've thought about a sunrise
you'd appreciate

(especially the kind
that lights up
some small drama
in the woods

A vine insisting it survive
say even if it kills
the tree it lives on
or cracks granite

and I wonder how and why)
I cannot tell you
how I wish you saw these things
for you would see

I swear I'll die remembering you
at three

sitting in an English garden
early one bright morning

so many
years ago
in your quilted bathrobe
and pink glasses

studying a flower
ordinary daisy I recall
nothing odd about it
I could see

from my upstairs bedroom window
You remained entranced
as windless light
engulfed you

wrapped you up
for always in my head
That kind of sunrise

Index

A Pal, 122

A Roof of Birds, 1

After They Shot Poor John Wilkes Booth, 69

Arousal, 2

Brighter Now, 119

Christ Church Cemetery, Philadelphia, 102

Come Again?, 111

Confession, 116

Dress Boy, 141

Dyad, 5

Elegy for Patrick, 7

Fat Kid, 138

Friend of Mine, 11

From the Poetry License Bureau, 126

Harbingers of the New Life, 13

Hot Shiskebab, 163

Hot to Trot, 121

How Many Times, 185

I Keep on Writing Poems, 184

I Want to Thank, 182

Inchoate Sunshine Cannot Tell, 14

Kid on a Bike, 101

Lately the Sunlight on Your Face, 131

Le Livre de M'Amie, *15*

LetMe Suggest the Following, *178*

Limericks, *16*

Lovesong, *17*

Man Who Played Piano, *19*

March Morning, *23*

Morton Street Pier, *24*

No Luck at All, *105*

Nones, *26*

Not That I Minded, *11*

Not to Have Failed, *29*

Not to Put Too Fine a Point on It, *145*

November, *30*

O Thank You, Lord, *32*

Others, *34*

Over and Over and Over, *137*

Pasadena Blonde, *153*

Passing in the Hall, *123*

Pedal to the Metal, *125*

Plat du Jour, *127*

Precis, *35*

Prose and the Passion, *36*

Raining, *103*

Ready or Not, *48*

Sacre du Printemps, *51*

Sext, *52*

So Here's What I Tell Her, 134

Sometime or Other, 171

Soon You Will Forget Your Own Name, 129

Spring Cleaning, 110

Tambourine, 54

Tanka, 180

The Approach, 56

The Counterfeiter's Tale, 81

The Girl in the Low-Cut Jeans, 169

The Pearl, 96

The Stars These Days, 77

The Wave, 58

These College Girls, 79

Thin Air, 95

This Poem Noise, 60

Tisha B'av Follies, 91

Two Haiku, 181

Vespers, 61

Walking Man, 175

We Knew Each Other, 62

West River Sundown, 63

What He Never Told Me, 153

What We Were Talking About, 167

When I Miss You, 173

You Get My Business Card, 132

About the Author

When he won the New York City Barton's Bonbonniere Passover Poetry Contest at the age of fourteen, Barry Sheinkopf's prize was a five-pound box of chocolates. He had a bad case of acne at the time and likes to say his career as a poet has gone downhill ever since. But he has continued to produce poems in a wide range of styes in the intervening decades, taking up technical challenges ranging from making traditional stanza and verse forms sound like free verse to his latest work, which attempts to capture the rhythms and absence of punctuation characteristic of email.

A crime novelist and essayist, Mr. Sheinkopf has, for over thirty years, headed The Writing Center in Englewood Cliffs, New Jersey, where he teaches writing, designs books through Bookshapers.com, and serves as publisher of Full Court Press. He has also taught for many years at the College of Staten Island. He is an active member of both Mystery Writers of America and the Authors Guild.

Mr. Sheinkopf lives in West New York, New Jersey, with his beloved wife, Eugenia Koukounas, and their two cats. He has two children, Susan and David, by a previous marriage.

This book has been set in Hoefler's *Requiem*,
derived from a set of inscriptional capitals
appearing in Ludovico Vicentino degli Arrighi's
1523 writing manual, *Il Modo de Temparere le Penne*.

www.ingramcontent.com/pod-product-compliance
Lightning Source LLC
Chambersburg PA
CBHW031143160426
43193CB00008B/232